APOSTOLIC CENTERS

God's Battle Stations

MIKE HERNANDEZ

Apostolic Centers God's Battle Stations Copyright © 2024 by Mike Hernandez

All rights reserved. This book or any portion thereof may not be reproduced or used in any manner whatsoever without the express written permission of the publisher except for the use of brief quotations in a book review or scholarly journal.

Book Published By: Beginning & Ending Publishing, LLC operating as BE Published.

First Printing: 2024

ISBN: 9798321763148

TABLE OF CONTENTS

Dedication 4
Endorsements 5
Forward 7
Introduction 11
New Wineskin 14
Apostles Are Commanders 19
1st Century Church Vs. American Church 29
Apostolic Centers Vs. Churches 46
Questions And Answers 63

DEDICATION

This book is dedicated to young pioneers who sense the call of God to warfare. I want to say you are not alone, and what you feel is not wrong! May this book awaken the young David's of our time.

ENDORSEMENTS

If you are Kingdom-Minded and interested in where the body of Christ is headed, this book will help you navigate the uncharted terrain called "The Future."
Dr. Deborah DeGar

Apostolic Centers: God's Battle Stations is excellent! It is a distinct and unique look at the differences between apostolic centers and churches. However, Pastor Mike Hernandez goes deeper and further than comparing the two types of ministries. Among other commendable highlights in the book, he has written powerfully about the power of the Holy Spirit. He has written in an anointed way about Paul's anointing as a spiritual warrior. He has also written with spiritual discernment about the leading role apostolic centers play in waging spiritual warfare. *Apostolic Centers: God's Battle Stations* is a must-read for builders of Apostolic centers and those who lead them.
Dr. Greg Wallace
Founder, The Relational Community

Apostolic Centers: God's Battle Stations is a must-read! This book serves as a tool for understanding the distinct differences between churches and Apostolic centers. In the Body of Christ, we are seeing an emergence of Apostles and Prophets like never before. In this book, Pastor Mike gives insightful, thought-provoking examples so that the reader can understand that in the modern-day church, God is calling for Apostolic hubs so that the focus can be Jesus-centered, Holy Spirit-led with an emphasis on equipping believers and sending them out to fulfill the great commission. This book is excellent for any leader who has an Apostolic grace upon their life and for any leader who may be in the building or rebuilding phase of ministry. The comparison and contrast of church vs. Apostolic centers will enlighten, challenge, and give understanding to any leader seeking change or guidance. As the Kingdom of God advances, we must have the language and knowledge of what is being pioneered in this modern-day. This book is sure to bring clarity and confirmation for the builder. Each page is inspired by the Holy Spirit and packed with scripture to get an understanding. I highly recommend this book to anyone leading God's people in any capacity.

Dr. Erica D. Montgomery, Author, and Pastor

FORWARD

Apostle Paul told us apostles and prophets are essential for the Church to function effectively.

"God has appointed in the church, first apostles, second prophets, third teachers, then miracles, then gifts of healings, helps, administrations, various kinds of tongues." (I Corinthians 12:28 NASB)

When Paul spoke of apostles being first in this verse, he used the Greek word prōtos, which means foremost (in time, place, order, or importance), first (of all). Paul reinforced the importance of apostles and prophets when he told the Ephesians that the Church was built upon the foundation of the apostles and prophets with Christ Jesus Himself, the Chief Cornerstone. *(Ephesians 2:20 AMPC)*

Unfortunately, since the days of the Roman Emperor Constantine I around AD 325, most of the Body of Christ has not been aware of the essential role apostles and prophets play in equipping the saints to fulfill their destiny. To fully equip the Church to fulfill the Great Commission, it takes all five of the "office gifts" Jesus gave to His Bride; apostles, prophets, teachers, evangelists and pastors. *(Ephesians 4:11-16)*. There is also a "sixth gift" Jesus gave His Bride, which activates the five "office gifts" to equip the saints to fulfill their destiny effectively; this gift is the one Jesus is continuously pouring out on our behalf – intercession. All six of these gifts are essential attributes of an apostolic center.

"Therefore He is able also to save to the uttermost (completely, perfectly, finally, and for all time and eternity) those who come to God through Him since He is always living to make petition to God and intercede with Him and intervene for them." *(Hebrews 7:25 AMPC)*

In Apostolic Centers—God's Battle Stations, Michael Hernandez has provided an excellent introductory discussion of a historical truth found in Scripture and the Church's first thousand years: Apostolic centers were and are part of God's plan to prepare His Bride for the great end-time harvest.

A passionate student of the Word of God and Church history will be interested in the impact of apostolic centers in Jerusalem, Antioch, Ephesus, Corinth, Rome, Iona, Ireland, and Scotland.

Through apostolic centers, every Christian could be trained and equipped to minister in their spiritual gifts with the power of the Holy Spirit. *(John 14:12 "...Truly, truly, I say to you, he who believes in Me, the works I do, he will do also; and greater works than these he will do; because I go to the Father....")* When this happens, the miraculous becomes common. In 195 AD, Irenaeus wrote, "prophetic words, tongues, and miracles of healings were common in the church." Then he added the Church frequently saw people raised from the dead through the prayers of the saints!

In the centuries after Constantine, a shroud of death spread across the Church! By the Sixth Century, the early Church only survived where the Roman armies could not enforce Constantine's edicts. The last remnant of the early Church was the Celtic Church in Scotland and Ireland because they had never been part of the Roman Empire, where apostles like Patrick, Columba, and many others continued to heal the sick, raise the dead, and equip the saints to minister! The Celtic Church operated in Ireland and Scotland well into the Eighth Century.

The Celts had an interesting strategy for their outreach—they built apostolic centers! Catholic historians called them "monasteries," but that is NOT what they were. Here, the Celtic priests married and had children. They moved into pagan territory and established the center as a beachhead. A monastery is a place to escape from the world and be alone with God. An apostolic center is a place to penetrate the world!

The Celts established Apostolic Worship Centers, which formed teams that maintained 24/7 praise and intercession for generations. These centers were Apostolic Training Centers that taught the Bible, intercession, and power ministry, and they sent out Teams to change the territory! They were not trying to escape from the world; these Apostolic centers were designed to penetrate the world with the Gospel! These were true Apostolic centers.

Jesus said, "If you continue in My Word, then you are truly disciples of Mine; and you will know the truth, and the truth will make you free." *(John 8:31-32 NASB)* In this book, Michael Hernandez has laid out some foundational Biblical truths that will open the door for seekers of Truth to be equipped to move into the authority Jesus intended for the sons and daughters of God to walk in. (Luke 10:19)

Mike masterfully presents the argument for apostles and prophets in our generation.

Indeed, suppose Jesus rose from the dead and is alive. In that case, apostles, prophets, teachers, evangelists, and pastors exist today because Jesus is the prōtos (foremost in time, place, order, and importance), apostle, prophet, teacher, evangelist, and pastor.

As Mike reveals in this book, throughout Scripture and church history, apostles and prophets have walked the Earth to assist with equipping and leading the Body of Christ to fulfill Heaven's mandate. Apostles function on a "spiritual continuum" ranging from "pure fatherly and motherly mentors" to "strategic generals," as the Holy Spirit directs the gift in them. In every case, true apostolic leaders equip the children of God to mature in the Father's grace so they can be sent to fulfill the redemptive purpose of God for their lives. *(Romans 12:6-8)*

I encourage you to ask the Holy Spirit to lead you in all Truth and equip you for the battle over the harvest fields in which you are called to war and labor. I send you to prosper and be in health as your soul prospers in the King of Glory!

Albert E. Hauck, PhD
President, Apostolic Intercessors Network

INTRODUCTION

Apostolic Hubs have existed since the first-century church began. Many have labeled them Apostolic Hubs, but my preference throughout the book is Apostolic Centers. Both centers and hubs are the same thing but are used interchangeably by Apostolic Leaders. My preference is to use center over hub. I've also incorporated the use of it into our ministry's name, FAM City Center, an emerging Apostolic center. I also refer to Apostolic Centers as God's Battle Stations.

Apostolic Centers are necessary. They change the concept of "Church" in America. Church in America consists of A Pastor who leads a community of people who come to listen to them speak every Sunday. They have programs in place and a timeframe set that must be met. Nothing is wrong with a program, but the problem arises when these programs replace God's presence. Many would get offended by this statement because none would say they do that, but how do we evaluate it? Later, I'll explain how Apostolic Centers do not necessarily operate this way.

Speaking of a main leader, this brings me to a primary reason Apostolic Centers are necessary: they are led by Apostles, not Pastors. This term is foreign to many because America is the home of Pastors. We are familiar with acknowledging Pastors, Teachers, and Evangelists, but Apostles and Prophets are very seldom accepted. This is unfortunate because the New Testament speaks much more about Apostles and Prophets than it does about Pastors. We must ask ourselves how can we use the term Pastor more if the Word of God mentions it less than the Apostle and Prophet. How did we arrive at such a place as this? It is a place where we do not accept the use of the titles and offices of the Apostle and Prophet. Some people deny their very existence.

Apostolic Centers have a structure, but it is flexible enough for God's New Wine to pour out. I want you to understand how necessary these Battle Stations are for the end times. Their programs are present but not more than the Presence of God. They have a main leader; however, they are not an entertainer but rather an equipper of the sheep to turn them into warriors. The senior leader does not do all the work but equips the people to do it as Ephesians 4 instructs. The Lord is raising up different Apostolic Centers worldwide with different purposes and distinct expressions, which will be explained in the following chapters. I hope you will understand the concept of Apostolic Centers and their necessity for today as God's End Time Answer.

APOSTOLIC CENTERS

God's Battle Stations

CHAPTER One

New Wineskin

DENOMINATIONS ARE DONE! What a crazy statement to make! This chapter is to help you lay aside your preconceived ideas and biased opinions. Lay everything aside, especially what you think I am going to say, but instead, trust the Holy Spirit to speak it to you. Only in doing so will you make the most out of this book.

What do I mean by denominations are done? I do not mean they no longer exist because they obviously do! I'm saying that God does not see denominations as we do. He only sees one Body, His Church, which He bought with His Blood. Throughout church history, many theologians have stated that God has been restoring biblical truths to The Body of Christ. The Apostle Luke says it this way in Acts.

"Whom Heaven must receive until the times of restoration of all things, which God has spoken by the mouth of all His holy prophets since the world began." Acts 3:21

We know that nothing is new under the sun (Ecclesiastes 1:9), so each truth has not been new to the Body of Christ but restored to its original intention. The issue was never in God restoring truths to His Church, but rather in the Church keeping up with each truth restored. Think about your cell phone, for example. Every so often, you will get a notification that says update. If you do not "Update," then more advanced technology keeps coming out while you stay stuck in something of the past. If you are not updated, then you become outdated. Many churches today are outdated because God has moved on with several restored truths, and they have refused them; this is known as denominationalism. Nothing is wrong with denominations; they are filled with people who love Jesus. The problem with them is that they represent their denomination more than they represent Jesus. I love the way Rick Joyner puts it, "Denominationalism is spiritual racism." You can go ahead and say ouch!

However, when you think about it, there is much truth to that statement! It is not ok to not hang out with a particular culture or race because they are not like you. People in like manner do this all the time with their denomination. If people do not believe a certain way or in a specific doctrine, they cut ties with them. That sounds like a gang to me. It is unfortunate but a reality in the Body of Christ. When I say

God is done with denominations, I'm saying we cannot keep pushing each other away when God seeks to unite His Church in these last days. Putting aside doctrinal differences is a sign of maturity for the greater good of Christ's Body. When we can finally come together and love each other more than our denominations, we can look like Christ's disciples.

Let me challenge you with this question. How many people do you talk to who disagree with you doctrinally? How many friends do you have whose beliefs and faith aren't like yours? We will always gravitate to those who agree with us, but can I propose something else to you? What if we all agreed to put aside our doctrinal differences and instead picked up our crosses? What impact could we make when we do something like this? Like I always say, you can be doctrinally correct but relationally wrong. If we believe in the major doctrines of the faith, such as salvation is by Christ alone and nobody can enter the Kingdom unless they are born again, and Jesus was born of a virgin and will return.

The secondary aspects of our faith, such as how we do baptisms, operate in gifts, placement of women in ministry, etc., can be something we lay down while we still decide to work together. The harvest is fast approaching and cannot be contained by any one denomination. If we think this is about our denomination, we live in pride, and God will humble the prideful! Rick Joyner stated, "If you are about to die, don't you think what you pray would be of the utmost importance to you?" When we read John, our Lord's Prayer was one of unity. Could the body of Christ dwelling in unity have been Jesus' heart's desire for us before He was crucified? We must ask ourselves how united are we with those who are part of different denominations. The Lord is calling out to His Body with one word in this hour: unity! He seeks to unite us like He is united as One with the Father. Are you willing to answer the call to unity?

Admonition To Every Denomination

I remember hearing a prophetic vision given by a man of God who saw angels flying to different churches. As they arrived at these churches, they wrote Ichabod, which means the Glory of God has departed. It shook me but resonated with me because when you become outdated, you lose God's Glory. Let me explain. It does not mean people are no longer saved or stopped loving Jesus. It means winning a new and emerging generation cannot be achieved without the Glory of God. His Glory is poured out on what Scripture calls new wine *(Matthew 9:17).* When God restores a specific truth to His Body, He is pouring out His Glory, and this is labeled as new wine. Each truth of the past was, at one-point, new wine, but as God kept pouring new wine into His Body, the older truths became old wineskins. Let's go back to the analogy of your phone to explain further. New wine is like having a new phone. Each time God pours out new wine in His Body, it is like you are purchasing a new phone. You can still have the older version, but it will not have the advanced capabilities of newer phones. In like manner, churches that remain stuck in old denominational truths without being updated will become old wineskins.

This is my admonition to all: we cannot win a new generation as old wineskins using old methods. As Rick Warren once stated, "God's message of the Cross always stays the same, but the methods change every generation." Are you willing to adjust to what God is doing here and now? Or will you become like Saul, who, through jealousy, envied the one God was raising up? It is righteous to honor the former, but embracing the new is imperative. What is God doing that is new in your day? Have you seen it? Can you identify it? Are you a part of it? Most of us treat God's truths like people treat leaving their homes as adults. It is estimated that most adults only move up to 15-20 minutes away from their upbringing. In the same way, many people who were raised by a specific denomination will never move away from that denomination to discover a that there is a world out there that they have yet to explore, but there is one, and they are missing out!

I challenge you to be open to the rest of this book as we dive into Apostolic Centers.

CHAPTER Two

Apostles Are Commanders

I remember hearing John Maxwell talk about leaders entering a room. He said, "The leader does not need to sit at the head of the table because wherever the leader sits are the head of the table." This is how an Apostle's presence is felt when they enter a place! When they show up, soldiers show up with them. They are honored, respected, and even feared. It reminds me of a Scripture in Acts 5.

"Yet none of the rest dared join them, but the people esteemed them highly." Acts 5:13

This statement was made right after Ananias and Sapphira dropped dead at the judgment of the Holy Spirit, as spoken by the mouth of Apostle Peter. As you might guess, no one dared join them after seeing the kind of authority God had granted them. As I heard Bishop Bill Hamon once say in a Conference, "People still do not think God kills people." In a war, there are casualties, but commanders in the highest of rankings give orders. Regarding Apostles, they are the highest-ranking people in God's Kingdom.

"And God has appointed these in the church: first apostles, second prophets, third teachers, after that miracles, then gifts of healings, helps, administrations, varieties of tongues." I Corinthians 12:28

As you can see, the Apostles being first shows they are first in rank and order in the Kingdom of God. They are first on the frontlines of war, which is why Jesus appointed only the twelve disciples and commissioned them as Apostles, not Pastors. I believe they did have a heart of compassion for people, but that came second to their heart of a lion, which sought to take territory away from an enemy. Our enemy, who roams around like a roaring lion, is the devil. Yet, God has commissioned last-day commanders called Apostles to oppose him in their time to take back territory. This brings us to a very interesting topic: spiritual warfare.

Spiritual Warfare

I previously mentioned that Apostles are on the frontlines of war. They are the ones who are not only giving orders but are being shot at by the enemy more than any other company of people. This is why Satan in Luke 22 asked to sift Peter like wheat. The word "sift" is a powerful word. I remember hearing Pastor Robert Morris explain that sift does not just mean asking like we think to ask for something with care. It means to demand and be granted permission to have. This is why Jesus said, "when you return" *(Luke 22:32)* because God permitted Satan to tempt Peter.

The point I am making here is that Satan attacked an Apostle whom Jesus was training. Can I suggest something to you that you never thought of? In the Gospels, I see Peter as the only one Satan asked to sift. Have you ever asked why? He did not ask for John or Mark. Why did he only ask for Peter? Some might say, well, it was because of his pride, this may be true, but I believe it is partially true. Let me explain. As I read the Gospel stories, I think all the young and immature Apostles had pride. Two scriptural proofs are that some of them wanted to call down fire from Heaven to kill people *(Luke 9:54),* while at another time, they were arguing about who was the greatest of them all *(Mark 9:34).* This sounds like pride to me! Back to the question. Why did Satan choose Peter to sift more than the others? I believe the answer is that Peter was the leader of the leaders. I find this true when he pridefully made the statement of not denying the Lord.

"But he (Peter) spoke more vehemently, "If I have to die with You, I will not deny You!" And they all said likewise." Mark 14:31

What Peter did, the rest of the Apostles followed. The Apostles followed Peter when he went fishing after denying Jesus.

"Simon Peter said to them, "I am going fishing." They said to him, "We are going with you also." They went out and immediately got into the boat, and that night they caught nothing." John 21:3

Peter had a great influence over the other leaders, which is why I believe Satan targeted him more than any other Apostle except Judas. This is to convey that there is a real enemy, and he is after leaders, mainly those whom God call Apostles. Let me share another important revelation of why I believe the enemy attacks Apostles so viciously.

Anointing To Advance

I want to call this term "the anointing to advance." In Jesus' words, He said GO! I want to return to the war analogy and speak of the infantry group. It comprises a small group of men whose mission is to advance on enemy territory. I like to look at these men as the Apostles. Going a bit further, if anyone is hurt or wounded during war, they are taken out and placed in a hospital to be nursed back to health. The people who care for them by bandaging their wounds and caring for their well-being are doctors. I like to see these people as Pastors. They are still part of the same team, yet their role and function are distinctly different. The infantry group is on the frontlines during the war, while the doctors are in a safe place away from the war. Both are still working very hard, but the infantry groups' possibilities of dying are much higher than doctors. Referring to rank is why Apostles are first in order. Their primary task is not to tend to the wounded but to advance the Kingdom of God over enemy territory. For this to happen, they must carry an anointing and authority from God to make them heavy carriers in the spirit realm, which brings me to another scriptural proof.

"These (Apostles) who have turned the world upside down have come here too." Acts 17:6

Having turned the world upside down is a heavy statement to make. As I mentioned at the beginning of this chapter, when a leader steps into a room, their presence is felt. In like manner, when an Apostle steps into the territory assigned by God, all of Heaven recognizes their authority! Rick Joyner quoted, "The first century Church started out with Apostles, and the last century church will close out with Apostles." For the Kingdom of God to advance to its fullest, it will be led by Apostles. There are no ifs, ands or buts about it! These people were born to lead!

Glory Over Goliath

As of this writing, we are in the year 2023 or 5784 in the Hebrew calendar. I gave our community the Word of the Lord, "this year's theme would be Greater Glory." One aspect of us stepping into Greater Glory is fighting against the Goliaths of our time. I believe every generation that emerges will have a showdown at some point in their life against a Goliath. Kings in the Old Testament can symbolize Apostles, while Priests can represent Pastors. Samuel anointed David as King, and the next thing he faced was Goliath. As God anoints emerging leaders, they will face champions in their city like Goliath. Scripture shows us the following from 1 Samuel 17.

"As he was talking with them, Goliath, the Philistine champion from Gath, stepped out from his lines and shouted his usual defiance, and David heard it. Whenever the Israelites saw the man, they all fled from him in great fear." 1 Samuel 17:23-24

As we can see, demonic champions are chanting in our cities. They have yet to be confronted by an anointed Apostolic leader! From this scripture above, we understand that people fled in fear, but the good news is that King David heard it and responded! He confronted the city's champion. I believe God is revealing Apostolic leaders who are hearing the enemy's defiance, and they will stand and confront him! When most of the people are fleeing from the battle, these people are running to it! I challenge you to seek to understand the demonic champions in your city. Who are they? Have those powers been confronted yet? Why are there still certain strongholds in your city? We cannot defeat an enemy we cannot see or, worse, do not believe even exists.

We can witness physical evil running rampant in our city, but we must identify the evil spirits operating in the heavenly realm. Many call this spiritual mapping. I encourage you to dive deep into this subject. Every city has different strongholds or strongmen that have tied up the souls of mankind in that region. Our mandate is to identify them, then expose them to dismantle them. Remember, we do not war against flesh and blood but against principalities and powers. Our weapons of warfare are mighty in God for pulling down strongholds, which is why we must study our enemy before we engage him. I believe David did this, and he understood that God would grant him victory through what he had been through previously. David told Saul the following:

"Your servant has killed both the lion and the bear; this uncircumcised Philistine will be like one of them, because he has defied the armies of the living God. The LORD who rescued me from the paw of the lion and the paw of the bear will rescue me from the hand of this Philistine." Saul said to David, "Go, and the LORD be with you." 1 Samuel 17:36-37

Likewise, Apostles today have been training in the background, just like David did with the bears and the lions. God is preparing them to face their Goliath. In this final showdown, the cities that have been tied up for so long will become revival hotspots all over the world! The Goliaths will not only be confronted but defeated by the least likely of people. Will you be one of them?

Let's Finish The Job

Have you ever asked yourself how could Goliath die with one little stone hitting him in the head? I always found this hard to believe until I understood two things. First, David made a decree, and second, I believe the stone carried the Glory of God. David made the decree written in scripture.

"This day, the LORD will deliver you into my hands, and I'll strike you down and cut off your head. This very day, I will give the carcasses of the Philistine army to the birds and the wild animals, and the whole world will know that there is a God in Israel. All those gathered here will know that it is not by sword or spear that the LORD saves; for the battle is the LORD's, and he will give all of you into our hands." 1 Samuel 17:46-47

David made a decree of God's judgment to the champion Goliath. These decrees are reserved for last-day Apostles because of the rank of evil over territories they will face. We all have authority to confront the enemy in our lives but only Apostles carry the authority to decree judgment over principalities. Goliath is an Old Testament principality, and David was the Apostle who decreed judgment over him. Second, we find the stone that took Goliath out.

"Reaching into his bag and taking out a stone, he slung it and struck the Philistine on the forehead. The stone sank into his forehead, and he fell facedown on the ground. So David triumphed over the Philistine with a sling and a stone; without a sword in his hand he struck down the Philistine and killed him." 1 Samuel 17:49-50

Going back to my question, how could this little stone kill such a huge man with one shot? We answered this question first by stating David made a decree of judgement but second, I suggested the stone carried the Glory of God. Let me explain. One of the words for Glory is "kabob," which can be translated as "weight." When we are under the anointing, we can move, but when we are under His Glory, we cannot stand! I believe God put the weight of His Glory on the stone the moment David slung it at Goliath. The moment it hit him, he fell and died. If you remember, the same thing happened to Ananias and Sapphira; they died when they lied in the Glory of God *(Acts 5)*. The Glory of God is a very serious matter! I want to discuss one more thing, and I will use the following passage of scripture for clarity.

"David ran and stood over him. He took hold of the Philistine's sword and drew it from the sheath. After he killed him, he cut off his head with the sword. When the Philistines saw that their hero was dead, they turned and ran." 1 Samuel 17:51

I know the above text might be a little graphic, but it is imperative to understand its significance. David did not stop when Goliath fell to the ground dead but went over, drew his sword from his sheath, and went off with his head! This shows me we can knock the enemy down but not out for good. Take, for example, an event we do where people get saved, delivered, and healed. We can say with certainty we took souls away from the kingdom of darkness, and we would be correct. However, if the champion of that city or region was not addressed, the lesser powers were scattered but will reemerge again under the principality's leadership. Remember the lesser of the Philistines gathered around their champion Goliath. This is what the lesser spirits, such as lust or pornography, do; they gather around the principality of Jezebel. To make it even easier to understand, it is like cutting weeds without removing the root. It is just a matter of time before it grows back! Apostles are the ones who will make the decrees of judgment over the champions of the city to make sure the enemy is defeated once and for all! The text above clearly shows that "when the Philistines saw their hero was dead, they turned and ran." As the principalities or champions of our city are addressed, the lesser powers will flee, and a great harvest will come and remain! Apostles, God's last-day commanders, will lead this charge.

CHAPTER
Three

1St Century Church Vs. American Church

    I love to read books and want to refute something I have heard many say over the years, "You cannot say what others have already said." Although I understand their point, I can't entirely agree with it for the following reasons. First, books have disciplined me more than any conference or school. People's whole lives of forty-plus years are put into a book you can read in a few hours. If this is not valuable to you, I do not know what is. I never place books over the book, which is the Bible, but I embrace learning from others and gleaning from their wisdom. You might be wondering why this chapter was started this way. In a book I am currently reading by Dr. Jonathan David, one of the most profound statements I have ever heard was this:

"You cannot walk in a new message until you have been baptized into the old order first."

He was referencing Jesus carrying the new message of the Kingdom of God, yet He was "first baptized" by John. Scripture tells us why He did it.

"And John tried to prevent Him, saying, "I need to be baptized by You, and are You coming to me?" But Jesus answered and said to him, "Permit it to be so now, for thus it is fitting for us to fulfill all righteousness." Then he allowed Him." Matthew 3:14-15

Jesus allowed John the Baptist to baptize Him, stating it was to fulfill all righteousness. It is my belief that any emerging leader who lacks honor for leaders who have paved the way for them are not fulfilling all righteousness. You will find several recommendations of people I recommend you listen to at the end of the next chapter. These are some of the people who have paved the way and have a proven model that has been tested over time. God cannot trust us with something new when we dishonor what has already been.

I Am A Practicing Theorist

When I read books, I intently evaluate each topic and subject. Throughout planting our ministry four years ago, I knew the Lord had called me to be an Apostle. I have shared with others that although I have the gift of an Apostle, I do not believe I walk in the office of one yet; however, I sense I am close. I want to be as honest as possible with you reading this book. Our ministry is becoming an Apostolic Center but is not quite there yet. I plan to write another book when we fully develop into an Apostolic Center. Why write this book? The answer is that I do not find many Apostolic Centers in my region or city, and I want to encourage people to learn about them. I am also connected to several proven Apostles who run Apostolic Centers. I have read a lot of material and learned over the years; I can give a basic overview of these centers. In conclusion, I would rather learn from a practicing theorist than one who is just a theorist. The following descriptions will help bring clarity to you moving forward.

1st Century Church Vs. American Church

We begin with a contrast of the two. When looking at the first-century church and our American church, do you notice any differences? I notice a lot of differences. We will point these out so as not to criticize but rather convict us on how far we have fallen from God's original model. It is right there in scripture, but we miss it! We begin by way of evaluation. This might step on many people's toes, but please know I do it out of love. Allow your thinking to be challenged through this list, and finish by evaluating yourself instead of defending your position. Can you do this for me? More importantly, can you do it for yourself and your ministry?

Here is the evaluation I would challenge your thinking on. How do we define success in ministry? Most would say attendance. We have a specific number of people coming, which makes us successful. However, is this true? I always ask myself if attendance means someone is truly saved, involved, or even in the right place. If attendance meant success, our city should be in revival because millions of people attend church every Sunday. We know this is not the case. Here is another thing people share that they believe makes their church successful.

People have facilities. Although this is a great thing to possess, this does not automatically mean success. In a recent conference, I shared what Barna Research discovered. Four thousand new churches open every year, while 7,000 churches close. As you can see, more churches are closing than they are opening yearly in America. You might think having a facility spells success would contradict this statement of statistics. Again, I am not saying buying a building is bad. I suggest challenging ourselves by asking if this is the only way to measure success or have we bought into this American idea if I do not have a building, I am not doing God's will or fulfilling God's call on my life. Think hard and long about this before you answer. We will go into some more analogies a little later, but for now, we will look at other reasons people believe their church is thriving.

Timing services, our God is One of order, but how much is too much order? Can we be so synchronized that there is no more room for the Holy Spirit to move? Could it be, as one person said, "The American Church would not even know when the Holy Spirit left because there are already programs in place."? Can we be bold enough to ask if we have replaced the presence of God with programs. Have we sold out His Presence by synchronizing everything and placing God in a box? He is the Creator of time; He can redeem time, but does He want to be placed on a time limit? How can we contain ourselves from a restroom break during a movie but get upset when the Pastor takes a little longer to minister to the people of God? Do you not see this as a problem? How can we show up early for the previews but not care when we are late for church? Where have our values gone?

Is the successful church a convenient one? Imagine somebody sharing how much they like your church because of its coffee but never once mentioned the Presence of God. I remember visiting a church on our sabbatical, and while the Pastor was preaching, I saw this long line. I did not know what it was until I approached it and got a better view. Immediately, I saw what was happening and people were getting coffee. Personally, I am not a fan of coffee, but my wife is, so please do not misunderstand me. I am not criticizing churches that offer coffee. People can come for coffee and stand in a long line for coffee but do not want to stay for prayer during ministry time. It sounds like we have catered to people to make things convenient for them; they even treat the church like movies. Again, this is my observation over the years when visiting different places. We can agree to disagree. I am challenging us through evaluation so we can seek to improve.

This last evaluation will probably be the most upsetting for most, and it is the prayer of salvation. Do we define success by how many people come to our altar every Sunday? I like how one man of God said, "People love to be touched but never change." Could it be the same people who keep coming to the altar leave only to come back the following Sunday with the same problem? Would this make their walk to the altar one of success, or could it be some of these people are taking God's grace in vain? Those who pray the prayer of salvation every Sunday yet persist in their sins Monday through Saturday. How do we explain that kind of behavior? Some might say well, it means they did not mean it. Ok, but they did pray after you told them to, right? They were following your instructions, correct? Again, I am not criticizing this because I honestly got saved this way. But it reminds me of Rick Joyner's statement, "We have turned our Gospel into come, and Jesus will save you from your problems, not your sins." We must do better by allowing Holy Spirit to convict people so conversions can happen instead of promising them problems will stop. Now, we will look at the New Testament Book of Acts and make practical suggestions on how the first-century church practiced.

Through this, you will see the differences between our American and first-century models.

The Power Of The First Century Church

Let's Start with prayer, the foundation.

"These all continued with one accord in prayer and supplication, with the women and Mary the mother of Jesus, and with His brothers." Acts 1:14

Continuing in prayer and with one accord shows me their unity in prayer. Every church leader would say that our church prays but ask some questions and make some evaluations. How often does our church pray for boldness during persecution, or does our church even receive any persecution? I will come back to this, but we will look at Acts chapter 4.

"And when they had prayed, the place where they were assembled together was shaken; and they were all filled with the Holy Spirit, and they spoke the word of God with boldness." Acts 4:31

Can we ask ourselves a few questions from this text? How many people leave our prayer meetings filled with the Holy Spirit? Second, how many leave our prayer meetings ready to preach the Gospel more boldly than before? The first-century church had this boldness, which I believe the American church lacks because our prayer meetings are the least filled gatherings. I once asked the Holy Spirit to send down fire from His Presence, and He said to me, "I cannot." I was stunned and proceeded to ask why. He said, "Because there are no bodies on My altar I can consume." I will never forget that statement, and it shook me to my core.

"I beseech you therefore, brethren, by the mercies of God, that you present your bodies a living sacrifice, holy, acceptable to God, which is your reasonable service." Romans 12:1

Interceding for others and our city is hard work. It takes a group of people who are willing to offer their bodies as a living sacrifice on the altar of the Lord. Until this happens, we will not be filled with His Spirit or be baptized in His boldness. Here is another core characteristic of the first-century church.

Speaking in Tongues

"Then there appeared to them divided tongues, as of fire, and one sat upon each of them. And they were all filled with the Holy Spirit and began to speak with other tongues, as the Spirit gave them utterance." Acts 2:3-4

The first thing the Holy Spirit did when He came to Earth was change the language of His people who were born again. There is much controversy around our heavenly language, but it is no coincidence that the enemy would do this because it produces much power. As leaders, we must ask ourselves how many people in our community have been baptized in the Holy Spirit with the evidence of speaking in tongues. Many Churches in America are like the disciples of John the Baptist in Acts 19. They are void of the of Holy Spirit.

"he said to them, "Did you receive the Holy Spirit when you believed?" So they said to him, "We have not so much as heard whether there is a Holy Spirit." Acts 19:2

How unfortunate that this statement is still being quoted in the church today. Some people do not even know there is a Holy Spirit who can baptize them into power and Heavenly language. It seems the Holy Spirit is the most neglected Person of the Trinity. Many are baptized into repentance but not into His power.

"And he said to them, "Into what then were you baptized?" So they said, "Into John's baptism." Acts 19:3

A countless number of people stop here instead of pressing in for more revelation. John's baptism was one of repentance but then came the promise of the Spirit. These men were disciples, but they had yet to receive His power. God is calling for an update for His church so we can receive everything the Holy Spirit came to deposit. Watch what happens next in their conversation with Apostle Paul.

"Then Paul said, "John indeed baptized with a baptism of repentance, saying to the people that they should believe on Him who would come after him, that is, on Christ Jesus."

When they heard this, they were baptized in the name of the Lord Jesus. And when Paul had laid hands on them, the Holy Spirit came upon them, and they spoke with tongues and prophesied." Acts 19:4-6

These disciples did not even know a Holy Spirit existed until Paul shared these truths with them. He baptized them in water, laid his hands on them, and they began to speak in tongues and prophesy! I pray for leaders like this to emerge who will help baptize the Body of Christ into His power. The kind of power the first-century church walked in is what we will highlight next.

"But you shall receive power when the Holy Spirit has come upon you; and you shall be witnesses to Me in Jerusalem, and in all Judea and Samaria, and to the end of the earth." Acts 1:8

Healing the Sick

The next question I pose as a challenge is how many people in our church walk in power. The kind of power to heal the sick and cast out demons. Some have believed this kind of power is only reserved for Apostles or leaders, but this is far from the truth.

"And these signs will follow those who believe: In My name they will cast out demons; they will speak with new tongues;" Mark 16:17

According to this passage, the prerequisite to walking in power is faith, not a position of leadership. Let me encourage you with two funny stories from my past as I began to grow in the power of God. I was invited to a middle school and shared a Word with a group of kids in the library. When I arrived, we waited outside the library doors because we arrived early. I was there with another one of my friends who I was discipling at the time. As I was looking at him and talking suddenly, I saw this image flash before me. It was a picture of a person with a cast on their leg.

I immediately told him God would heal somebody today with a cast on. He looked at me stunned but said ok. As we entered the library, we looked at all the kids to see if any had casts on their legs. We did not find any, so I was confused about the vision I had of a cast. The teacher then introduced me and invited me up to share. When I was about to speak up, the doors to the library opened, and everyone turned around. Sure enough, a young girl on crutches with a cast on her leg entered the door. I was so shocked and excited that I yelled, "sister, God is going to heal you today!". Of course, she looked at me puzzled and, quite frankly, probably thought I was a bit weird as I yelled this out of excitement.

I continued to share my brief message and asked her, "Can I pray for you?" She said yes and got closer to me so I could lay my hands on her leg. By this time, the teachers and students gathered around us as she explained how she had broken her ankle while playing volleyball. By this time, I was sweating and completely nervous because I thought, what if she does not get healed? I had such faith, right? I decided to go for it and started to speak healing over her ankle. Guess what? Nothing happened. I was shocked, thinking that God was not hearing me. I looked pretty foolish and felt embarrassed right now. I proceeded to pray again, and guess what happened the second time? Absolutely nothing. I even asked the girl, "Do you feel anything?" She said no! I was like oh Lord Jesus, help me! Suddenly, I got bold and said to her remove your cast. She looked at me strangely but then did as I asked. The moment I stretched out my hand to touch her ankle, she immediately screamed. I was so scared I jumped up and backed off her because I thought I had hurt her ankle. She rose, started screaming I am healed, and began jumping on her ankle. The library erupted in praise as the girl kept screaming, "I am healed!". She then started weeping, ran to hug me, and thanked me for praying for her. As the school bell rang, we all watched her walk away, waving at us with her crutches in her hand. God is good!

The second funny story is when I attended a prayer night in our old ministry. We used to host these prayer nights every Friday night. During this time, I watched many videos on evangelism and moved boldly toward the power of God. I remember watching this video about people's legs being stretched out because one leg is shorter. It intrigued me because you cannot make that stuff up. You could see people's legs growing out on camera, so I was amazed! As we took a brief break during the prayer night, a young girl came up to me to pray for her back because it was hurting. I immediately remembered the YouTube video and said no, sister, your back is hurting because one leg is shorter than the other! Let me pause here and say I do not recommend you do this with every person who has back problems. I think God was gracious with my ignorance and set things up perfectly for me to grow my faith. Now, back to my story. I sat her down, and sure enough, one leg was shorter than the other. I then told her we would command the shorter leg to grow to match the other. I remember her saying, "Mike, are you sure about this?" I declared with confidence, of course, because I saw it on YouTube!

Shout out to Todd White for encouraging my faith with his healing videos! I pressed in and said in Jesus Name and before I could even say grow, she screamed, and I backed away. Immediately she felt heat in her leg and felt all kinds of pressure as her leg grew out. She jumped up and started screaming, praising God, and sharing with everyone. We all stopped praying and began to worship God for working a miracle in this young girl's life. God is good! I hope these two stories help you to see God's power is not reserved for people in positions but for those who believe in Him and His Word.

Deliverance

The last thing I want to share about this is from a conference we hosted last year called Sharpen Your Sword. In this conference, we highlighted how spiritual warfare is the most undermined ministry while inner healing and deliverance are the most neglected. I do not believe demonic spirits can possess Christians, but I do believe they can oppress them. Many misinterpret the context, assuming possession means ownership, but this is not true. The literal meaning of possession in Greek (daimonizomai) means to gain a master over. So, do I believe demons can own Christians? Absolutely not! But can demons gain mastery over Christians who have open doors in their lives? Absolutely yes! Let me challenge you not to neglect these two areas of inner healing and deliverance. It is part of what Jesus calls the children's bread (Matthew 15:26). Now, we will discuss the last characteristic, which is persecution.

Persecution

We can ask a few questions: how often does our church receive persecution? How frequently are our leaders accused of things which are not true? When I read the New Testament Book of Acts, it is filled with persecution. How often does America experience this? This is not to say there has been none in our country, but overall, we are safe and secure by a long shot compared to Third World countries. We will start with accusation which cause disruptions with a move of God. Scripture says.

"But when the Jews saw the multitudes, they were filled with envy; and contradicting and blaspheming, they opposed the things spoken by Paul." Acts 13:45

A great way to assess a work is by asking how often it is opposed. As we can see in the text, the multitudes were gathering for the kind of authority with which Paul spoke, and a spirit of envy was aroused. People stay away from ministries that bring much conflict when they should be running to those kinds of ministries. Let's look at the following passage of scripture.

"Then Jews from Antioch and Iconium came there; having persuaded the multitudes, they stoned Paul and dragged him out of the city, supposing him to be dead." Acts 14:19

You would think Paul would catch a break, but he never did. The people who once listened to him were the same ones who began to stone him. The enemy used the religious Jews to turn the crowd Paul was reaching to turn against him. It is these kinds of accusations, as Maldonado says, are Satan's highest forms of attacks. That is why I asked the question, how often are your leaders accused of something that is not true? For the first time in four years of planting our ministry, my wife and I decided to count how many accusations we have faced, particularly myself. We counted fifteen! Which comes to about four people a year! None of them remained in our ministry, yet we still carry several scars from all the hurt they caused us. I always find encouragement in the scripture because after Paul was supposedly dead, look at what happened.

"However, when the disciples gathered around him, he rose up and went into the city. And the next day he departed with Barnabas to Derbe." Acts 14:20

Paul did not die, and he did not stay down or quit! He rose right back up and continued the mission God had called him to. Perhaps this is why the underground church in China experienced such amazing growth. They are not afraid of dying for the Lord. I sense they genuinely believe this passage of scripture.

"Precious in the sight of the Lord Is the death of His saints." Psalms 116:15

How can saints' dying be pleasant in the Lord's sight? The answer is that in the same way His Son laid down His life for us, we can lay down our lives for Him. Scripture teaches that this kind of people will experience a "better resurrection."

"Others were tortured, not accepting deliverance, that they might obtain a better resurrection." Hebrews 11:35

If we are going to walk in what the first-century church did, we must do some serious evaluating moving forward. There is much more I could highlight, but this is sufficient. I challenge you to assess the following:

1. Prayer and Unity.

2. Walking in power and boldness.

3. The ability to withstand persecution.

CHAPTER Four

Apostolic Centers Vs. Churches

Let me begin by saying Apostolic Centers are in no way better than Churches, likewise Apostles are than Pastors. We are the Body of Christ, and God has designed it so that we all need each other. When we truly value diversity we will see real unity. We're all different, so I am not suggesting one model fits all. Let me share with you what one man of God I highly respect named C. Peter Wagner discovered after evaluating the body of Christ. While he was still alive, he ran an Apostolic Network of Apostles, and each of them was asked whether they went to Bible college or seminary and how they conducted their discipleship within their community. The results he received were astounding! The first thing he noticed was that those who had not gone to seminary were the ones who had the largest churches. I will not even touch on that point. You can draw conclusions from it. The second, my main point, is that everyone was doing discipleship differently than others. This is why I do not appreciate people selling models to the church as if success is guaranteed when they do this. I believe principles are all-inclusive, but processes are not. Every process for every community is different, and it should be that way. This does not mean we change the message of the Gospel and compromise, but we adjust methods and structures based on the culture of the people we are reaching. I share all this to say each Apostolic Center will be different, just as every church is. No one model fits all, and I will never say it does. We are unique as leaders, and God will use this uniqueness to bring about a distinct expression of Himself for our generation. However, there are fundamental similarities in every Apostolic Center and Church as there are differences, and this is what we will now go through. After reading this, I hope you will understand which one you are part of, and which one God has called you to be a part of. We will start briefly with the similarities. They are easy to identify.

Both Apostolic Centers and Churches host services once a week. They both have times of worship during service and then hear the Word of God preached. There are no differences in this aspect at all. Both find a place to meet for this to happen, whether in a facility or home. Again, there are no differences between the two. Both have times of prayer at the end of the service so people can receive ministry from the Holy Spirit by way of the Pastor or leaders who are present. Lastly, they both are bonded through fellowship to grow in friendship and relationships. From somebody looking on from the outside in, you might be unable to tell the difference between an Apostolic Center and the church until you take a closer look. We will do this now as we share distinct key differences between the two.

1. Apostolic Center's message is more on the Kingdom than the church.

When you enter an Apostolic Center, its mission focuses on advancing the Kingdom of God, not church attendance. To say it another way, you can have many people coming, yet the Kingdom is still not advancing among you. Remember, Jesus changed the world with twelve Apostles, although thousands gathered around Him. The atmosphere of an Apostolic Center is pregnant with movement and activity from the Spirit of God. People are stirred to move and push forward to gain a deeper ground in their purpose. Church are those whom God has called out for a specific mission, while the Kingdom is what they carry with them wherever they go. They understand:

"nor will they say, 'See here!' or 'See there!' For indeed, the Kingdom of God is within you." Luke 17:21

The Kingdom is the domain of the King, and where these people go, the King's Presence goes with them. Shifting the people's mindsets from church to Kingdom is the assignment of an Apostolic Center. Much of America is centered on going to church when we should exercise the dominion of the Kingdom of God. The Apostolic Center will gear its messages to advance the Kingdom of God, while a church will gear its messages toward the community of people who attend. One will grow and expand, while the other will maintain weekly attendance. Another way to put it is people from an Apostolic Center care more about losing the Presence of God than they do people. They understand that without the presence of God, any person who did come would not have the power to change. It is only through the message of the Kingdom that the King will come.

2. An Apostle, not a board, governs Apostolic Centers.

This point might be the most shocking; let me quote C. Peter Wagner again. He stated, "The greatest distinction of Apostles more than any other aspect is not their ability to plant churches, but the designation of the Holy Spirit's authority to one individual." To clarify this, we can look at the Book of Acts from when they had the city council in Jerusalem. The issue was concerning the Gentiles and what they were supposed to do now that the Holy Spirit was being poured out upon them. The Apostles gathered to discuss this; imagine the weight of this meeting.

"Then all the multitude kept silent and listened to Barnabas and Paul declaring how many miracles and wonders God had worked through them among the Gentiles. And after they had become silent, James answered, saying, "Men and brethren, listen to me:" Acts 15:12-13

Many did not want to hear this profound and remarkable statement: "listen to me." Many Prophets, Evangelists, and Apostles were present at this meeting, but after hearing everyone, one man got up and said, "Listen to me." He made the final call, and all was settled with no disputes arising, and voting was not deemed necessary. To go even further, can I state James, who made the call, did not even go on the journey with Paul and Barnabas, yet they still heeded his decision! It is because an Apostle spoke up who everyone knew the Holy Spirit had designated the authority to and give the final verdict. The result was everyone followed. This, by far, is probably the most distinct difference between your everyday church and an Apostolic Center. The final decision is left in the hands of a man or woman who is an Apostle, not to a board of elders.

3. Apostolic Centers have an Apostolic Team, not a board of elders.

Looking at the book of Acts as our compass, we can see that Paul's team was Apostolic in nature. Although they did appoint elders, he only did so after the work was done, and he went on to his next assignment from God. Nowhere do we find elders governing Apostle Paul, but we do find Apostle Paul ordaining elders and giving orders to other Apostles. Here are a few examples.

"So when they had appointed elders in every church and prayed with fasting, they commended them to the Lord in whom they had believed. And after they had passed through Pisidia, they came to Pamphylia." Acts 14:23-24

We see here that Paul and his team appointed elders to the Lord in every church they had planted. Their time there was up. God was calling them elsewhere to start a new work, the very thing Apostles are destined to do. Here is another example:

"For this reason I left you in Crete, that you should set in order the things that are lacking, and appoint elders in every city as I commanded you" Titus 1:5

Appoint elders in every city as I commanded you. Wow, that sounds a lot like "listen to me"! But when you understand Apostles and Apostolic authority, you understand they are commanders seeking to occupy the territory they just gained through spiritual warfare. Paul instructed younger Apostles to occupy territory by establishing leaders in those churches. Paul had other Apostles on his team, but everyone knew Paul was the lead Apostle.

"When Silas and Timothy came from Macedonia, Paul devoted himself exclusively to preaching, testifying to the Jews that Jesus was the Messiah" Acts 18:5

In Acts 18:1-5, we find Paul described as a tent maker and becoming acquainted with the newest members of his team, Priscilla and Aquila. Verse five then shows us when the rest of his team showed up; he left making tents and devoted himself exclusively to preaching. This shows us Paul's ability to be bi-vocational but also proves his dependency and alignment with his Apostolic team. He could not devote himself exclusively to preaching until his team arrived. Thank God for divine relationships He sends our way.

4. Apostolic Centers have a commissioned Apostle, not a board that votes.

Most churches in the west are governed by a board that decides to hire rather than receive a sent person. I want to share two passages of scripture regarding this.

"Paul, an apostle—sent not from men nor by a man, but by Jesus Christ and God the Father, who raised him from the dead" Galatians 1:1

No man can call himself an Apostle or choose to be one, if he does, he is operating illegally in the spirit. As Maldonado says, "Our calling God chooses, but our career we choose." Sadly, many churches consider Pastoring a career, so they find a different church when things are not going well. This is not how it should be.

It isn't easy to truly depend upon a Pastor who we sense will not be with us for long. This is why God does not hire people; He calls people! Then He commissions them. Let's look at another scripture.

"As they ministered to the Lord and fasted, the Holy Spirit said, "Now separate to Me Barnabas and Saul for the work to which I have called them." Then, having fasted and prayed, and laid hands on them, they sent them away." Acts 13:2-3

People who lead Apostolic Centers understand this text very well. They live for the day God commissions them for the work He had set them apart for. They are not interested in being hired by man because they understand God has called them. A salary does not control them because a mission rather than money motivates them. This is not to discredit Pastors who labor hard, but it is to challenge our thinking and not see our work as a duty but rather a calling. We will do one grudgingly, while the other we will perform excellently. If we do not think men can appoint men, we must think again. Scripture gives an example of this:

"I know your works, your labor, your patience, and that you cannot bear those who are evil. And you have tested those

who say they are apostles and are not, and have found them liars" Revelation 2:2

If Jesus commended the Church of Ephesus for calling out certain men who claimed to be Apostles but were false, we must conclude other men placed them there, or worse, they put themselves there. When we operate in an Apostolic Center, the understanding of an Apostle who was sent to those people is understood to be a lifetime. The Apostle isn't going anywhere unless God sends them elsewhere, but even if this happens, you can be assured that godly leadership will be positioned before that time comes.

5. Apostolic Centers engage more in warfare than an everyday church.

This last one is my favorite one because I am a fighter. I always tell people our community is filled with Peters. I honestly think I have a special grace on my life to Pastor, some of the most difficult people. I believe Peter got on Jesus' nerves. Yet, Peter was the only one who Jesus gave keys to the Kingdom. Peter was loud, violent, prideful, and made many mistakes, but he was the one who led the way in the New Testament. People will follow Peters because they are not afraid to step out! Amen to that. We will look at a passage concerning Peter to bring home the point. Apostolic Centers are engaged in greater warfare than your everyday church.

"Peter was therefore kept in prison, but constant prayer was offered to God for him by the church. And when Herod was about to bring him out, that night Peter was sleeping, bound with two chains between two soldiers; and the guards before the door were keeping the prison. Now behold, an angel of the Lord stood by him, and a light shone in the prison; and he struck Peter on the side and raised him up, saying, "Arise quickly!" And his chains fell off his hands." Acts 12:5-7

The question I want to ask is, what kind of prayers were being offered to God for Peter? The beginning of this chapter starts off with James being martyred, so Peter was next in line. This positioned the church to do what we call spiritual warfare on behalf of God's Apostle. This kind of warfare against the spirit of death caused a miracle to occur when an angel of the Lord appeared, and Peter's chains fell off.

God sets up these Apostolic Centers as places to engage in battle with the enemy so the Kingdom of God can advance. Much of what happens in the Earth realm depends upon the intercession we make in the heavenly realm. The group of people interceding for Peter proved we can overcome death miraculously! Never stop praying for your leaders! I want to bring to your attention 1 Corinthians 15:32.

"If, in the manner of men, I have fought with beasts at Ephesus" 1 Corinthians 15:32

In scripture, beasts symbolize demons. Genesis 3 tells us the serpent was more cunning than any beasts of the field. I do not believe Paul was fighting people but demonic powers that were constantly opposing him. He references Ephesus, which in Acts 19 gives us an even clearer picture of how much warfare Apostles are called to engage in.

"Moreover you see and hear that not only at Ephesus, but throughout almost all Asia, this Paul has persuaded and turned away many people, saying that they are not gods which are made with hands. So not only is this trade of ours in danger of falling into disrepute, but also the temple of the great goddess Diana may be despised and her magnificence destroyed, whom all Asia and the world worship." Acts 19:26-27

This is one of the most profound statements in the New Testament validating an Apostle's authority. This is the reason the enemy hated Paul so much. His authority to invade territories and weaken forces of darkness was so powerful that the entire city went into an uproar. Ephesus became one of Paul's battle stations, but it was established when much spiritual warfare was achieved. In Acts 19, we also find God doing unusual miracles through the hands of Paul to set people free.

"Now God worked unusual miracles by the hands of Paul, so that even handkerchiefs or aprons were brought from his body to the sick, and the diseases left them and the evil spirits went out of them." Acts 19:11-12

Continuing to read Acts chapter 19, we then find another level of darkness being confronted in witchcraft.

"And many who had believed came confessing and telling their deeds. Also, many of those who had practiced magic brought their books together and burned them in the sight of all. And they counted up the value of them, and it totaled fifty thousand pieces of silver. So the word of the Lord grew mightily and prevailed." Acts 19:18-20

We can conclude that God used Paul first to get evil spirits out of individuals through unusual miracles. We then see how God used him to break the powers of witchcraft in a region. Paul was caught in a riot because the principality named the goddess of Diana was weakened by Paul, turning many to the faith (Acts 19:26-27). Other than in the ministry of Apostles and Prophets, we do not see God allowing this kind of warfare. When entering an Apostolic Center, this kind of warfare is not unusual but usual to the people because they understand their leaders' commissioning to the city.

We will now recap the following truths from comparing Apostolic Centers and Churches.

Apostolic Centers and churches both have the following:

1. Worship

2. The preaching of the Word

3. Ministry time to receive prayer.

4. Attend weekly gatherings, whether in facilities or at home.

5. Relationships and fellowship bond both together.

Apostolic Centers and Churches have differences:

1. Apostolic Center's message is more on the Kingdom than the church.

2. Apostolic Centers are led by an Apostle, not a board of deacons.

3. Apostolic Centers have an Apostolic team, not a board of elders.

4. Apostolic Centers have a commissioned Apostle, not a board that votes.

5. Apostolic Centers engage more in warfare than an everyday church.

To conclude this chapter, I thought it necessary to give you another way of contrasting Apostles and Pastors. This will be useful for simple evaluation and reflection. Some Pastors unknowingly function as Apostles but do not recognize it, and some don't understand it. I want to give you some basic guidelines for moving forward, which will help relieve your Pastor from unnecessary expectations. Sometimes, people can expect their leader to function as something they are not. Doing this will only set us up for disappointment because we assumed God sent us a Pastor when He sent us an Apostle or vice versa. I will also attach the rest of the evaluations contrasting Apostolic Centers and Churches for your personal reflection and study.

Please remember that this does not imply that Apostles and Apostolic Centers are better than Pastors and Churches. We all need one another. This information will help you understand the distinct differences of each as we learn to appreciate one another's expressions. May you be a blessing wherever the Lord calls you.

Churches Vs. Apostolic Centers Contrasts

1. Churches emphasize members, and Apostolic Centers emphasize disciples.

2. Churches emphasize sheep, and Apostolic Centers train sheep into shepherds.

3. Churches emphasize sermons, whereas Apostolic Centers emphasize revelation.

4. Church emphasizes attendance, and Apostolic Centers emphasize training.

5. Churches focus on maintaining, and Apostolic Centers emphasize movement.

6. Churches sing songs, while Apostolic Centers emphasize warfare worship.

7. Churches emphasize gatherings, and Apostolic Centers emphasize sending.

8. Churches focus on the service, and Apostolic Centers demonstrate the supernatural.

9. Churches emphasize facilities, and Apostolic Centers emphasize Heaven Blueprints.

Pastors Vs. Apostles Contrasts

1. Pastors keep sheep. Apostles send them.

2. Pastors care for the flock. Apostles bring correction to the community.

3. Pastors focus on people. Apostles primary focus is on assignment.

4. Pastors help to nurture. Apostles focus on maturing.

5. Pastors love to comfort people. Apostles enjoy aligning people.

6. Pastors stay in maintenance mode. Apostles stay in constant movement.

7. Pastors care for the wounded. Apostles lead the community into war.

8. Pastors keep the territory. Apostles obtain the territory.

9. Pastors have money management. Apostles produce wealth.

After reading the contrasts, I am sure you might think I do both of those and have seen my Pastor do this. You might even say I have seen my church function in those capacities, but it is still called a church. Let me remind you there are instances where both Churches and Apostolic Centers function similarly. I am not trying to show how one is better or lesser than the other, but I intend to give you a clearer picture of how each one operates so that you can better understand your leader and the ministry you are part of. This can even open the door for healthy conversations with your team or Pastor. I will go into more detail in my second volume, but for now, this is an excellent start for those who need to become more familiar with Apostles and Apostolic Centers.

CHAPTER
Five

Questions And Answers

It would be beneficial to close out this book to answer some questions. My desire through this Q & A is to do the following:

1. *I want to educate people because my heart desires to see more Apostolic Centers in my region.*
2. *I desire God's government to take its proper place in the Body of Christ. Without proper order, I do not think we can sustain the coming Harvest.*
3. *My heart is to see the church get updated in the things of God.*

Much of what we see today is outdated religion. God's heart is for us to be at the center of His will in every generation. I pray this last chapter will be an eye-opener of revelation that can take people to God's will of destination.

Who keeps the Apostle accountable?

I want to start here because the Apostle's authority is a very serious matter. Who do Apostles submit to? You might even feel a certain way about someone possessing that much power. Is it safe or right to have? It is a valid thought and a great question, so allow me to answer this way. First, the Apostle is accountable to God like every other Prophet, Evangelist, Pastor, and Teacher. We must remember that if God raised someone up, He can bring someone down. Accountability is more about a heart issue than it is about proper placement in a church's bylaws. I am in total agreement with the church's bylaws, but over the years, people have rejected them and continued in their sin. How does that happen, and how do we fix it? Let me suggest this to everyone.

The focus of longevity in a position of power is a willingness to yield to God and heed the counsel of others. A true Apostle carries the fear of the Lord and a servant's heart. They use their authority to build up and not to tear down. They desire to see the maturity of the Body of Christ. Each Apostle is in alignment with other Apostles, thus producing genuine submissions to one another. We see this in scripture where Paul aligned with Barnabas and Silas in the work of God. Every Apostle works in synergy with other Apostles and willingly puts themselves under mutual submission.

Because the Apostle's authority is so strong, it only makes sense to have them submit to another Apostle. Another pioneer would best understand a pioneer. Networks are crucial to be part of because they are made up of godly relationships. True submission comes out of these godly relationships. Each Apostle builds that bridge with one whom they know God has called them to align with. It is through this mutual submission that all are held accountable for upholding the highest standards of character amongst each other.

Should I join an Apostolic Center?

I would never suggest someone leave their church to join something they believe is a trend in the Body of Christ. We are not called to follow trends but the Lord. From my understanding of study, Apostolic Centers started being restored in early 2012. Remember, it is not something new the Lord is doing but restoring the model that's always been there. I suggest that people plan a visit to see one in person. It opens your eyes to see something you have never seen, especially in its maturity. Here are some people and some websites I encourage you to visit:

Apostle Chuck Pierce with Glory of Zion. Over the years, I have heard Prophets speak, and this is the most advanced Apostolic Center on earth today. We will allow you to judge that, but this is where my Apostle and I are aligned. For more information visit ***www.gloryofzion.org***

Apostle Al Hauck, who ordained me and my wife. His ministry in New York functions as an Apostolic Center. For more information visit **www.shcfellowship.org**

Apostle Alain Caron who also wrote an amazing book called, *"Apostolic Centers - shifting the church, transforming the world."* He was commissioned along with my Apostle by Chuck Pierce.

Apostle Che Anh from California. He has an Apostolic Network called HIM (Harvest International Ministries.) For more information visit *www.harvestrock.church*

Apostle Rick Joyner. What impacted me is how they have a fully accredited private school from kindergarten to twelfth grade. They have annual conferences to teach people how to start private schools, and home-schooling. For more information visit *www.Morningstarministries.org*

Each person carries a distinct expression of the Kingdom of God. As you plan your visit you will see the uniqueness of each one and better appreciate Gods diversity in His Body.

How can I talk to my Pastor ?

My first suggestion would be to do your research and do due diligence of study. Gather as much information as you can and go over it until you grasp a solid concept to communicate. Remember that the book you read came after four years of study, prayer, and research. I have read thousands of pages and listened to hundreds of hours of material. Only then could I grasp a concept worth communicating with an audience like you. If you are serious about speaking to your Pastor about this, do the work and pay the price.

Second, I would suggest praying for your Pastor's heart and your attitude when you speak to him. Do not go in there trying to convince him but trust the Holy Spirit to speak through you. Your focus should not be to persuade but only to share what you have learned. Leave the rest up to God, and do not get upset if your Pastor does not receive. If God led you there, you submit and learn all you can from the man or woman of God, you are under.

Should my church become an Apostolic Center?

If this is your question, I would advise you to read Apostle Alain Caron's book, which I put on question two. He shares how his ministry shifted from a church to an Apostolic Center in two years. It was not easy, but he shares how it was worth it. Not everyone is called to do this, but those who are interested in shifting will find his book extremely helpful as it guides you step by step.

Should I start an Apostolic Center?

Let me say this loud and clear: never start something God did not initiate! I remember watching Space Jam as a kid, and the moment the movie finished, I went outside to play basketball! I was not called to be a professional basketball player, but I was inspired to play the game. Planting an Apostolic Center is not a game. You may be inspired to do something but must get clarity of a calling versus an inspiration. Those who are inspired by a work but not called to start one, God will assign you to those who are. You must trust your inspiration was God's calling to assist, not to start. People can get these confused due to immaturity and start something God never called them to.

How do we know someone is called to do this?

First, there will be a sure call of God in their lives, as confirmed by real, proven Apostles. It does not matter much of what you say when it has not been validated by those who are valid. It is like a young kid saying he wants to be a professional baseball player. This kid must be validated by those who are valid professional baseball players. Let me repeat: You cannot validate yourself in something. You can feel called to it, but only those who have been through it can validate you.

Second, God will give you supernatural alliances. These are spiritual fathers and mothers to you in the faith. Not only will they validate you, but God will speak to them to commission you. We find this event happening in Acts 13. God will use other Apostles and Prophets to set you apart for His assigned work. We all have Divine authority from

Heaven, but we must also have the endorsement of His delegated authority on earth. You cannot have one without the other, or you will be operating illegally!

Last, you will find what Apostle Alain Caron calls in his book "Apostolic Attraction." This means God will draw men to the man to whom He gave His mantle. For example, God gave David His mantle for Kingship, and the next thing we see is God gathering the mighty men to David. It is God Who calls, and it is God Who draws. There is a major difference in networking skills versus apostolic attraction. Refrain from getting confused and thinking you are called. One is used by way of talent, while the other is used by way of spiritual governance. Your talent can gather a group of people, but only an apostolic alignment can transform them. This is how you can tell people started something God never initiated because people gather but are never transformed. Their ministry was a deployment of marketing, not one of commissioning. Be careful and get clarity and confirmation before starting something of major significance.

Thank you for finishing this book. My prayer is that it was educational, challenging, and encouraging all at the same time. I want to leave you with a prophetic exhortation from the Lord from the story of King David right when he was about to fight Goliath.

"Then Saul gave David his own armor—a bronze helmet and a coat of mail. David put it on, strapped the sword over it, and took a step or two to see what it was like, for he had never worn such things before. "I can't go in these," he protested to Saul. "I'm not used to them." So David took them off again." 1 Samuel 17:38-39

I believe that as Apostolic Centers emerge, a religious spirit of Saul will come forth. David's reply still speaks today, "I am not used to them." I think of people I have met over the years who are no longer used to church as usual. They can no longer stand the predictability of synchronized services. They know there is a battle ahead, and doing things the synchronized way is not going to work for them anymore. They do their best to honor the former but can no longer wear their armor. It is time for them to pick up and put on their own.

"He picked up five smooth stones from a stream and put them into his shepherd's bag. Then, armed only with his shepherd's staff and sling, he started across the valley to fight the Philistine." 1 Samuel 17:40

Apostolic Centers are emerging that will release young David's into their destinies! In these places, they will be trained for war and able to pick up their battle weapons. David had five smooth stones, which I believe symbolized God's strategy for his victory. It is up to you to decide which armor you will wear, but know the right choice will be found in what David did when scripture says he started across the valley to fight.

Then, armed only with his shepherd's staff and sling, he started across the valley to fight the Philistine." 1 Samuel 17:40

I hope to see you on the battlefield!

Made in the USA
Columbia, SC
07 May 2024

35371341R00039